D0430056

Rivet Your Readers
with
Deep Point of View

Jill Elizabeth Nelson

© 2012 by Jill Elizabeth Nelson

All rights reserved.
This handbook may not be reproduced in whole or in
part without express written permission or contractual
arrangement with the author.

ISBN-13: 978-1470063856
ISBN-10: 1470063859

Table of Contents

Introduction

Have you ever read a book that melded your mind with the main character's psyche? No vague sensation of an invisible narrator inserted itself between you and the point-of-view character. Line by line, scene by scene, you lived in that central character's head. Even if the story was not written in first person, the hero or heroine's every experience became yours, and your reading pleasure intensified. Why? How did this happen? What did the writer do to gain this effect?

The technique is called Deep Point of View. In this handbook, we'll plumb the depths (pun intended) of this fun and fundamental skill.

Warner Brothers employs a little blurb in promotion of their Blu-ray movies: "This is how our movies are meant to be—lived!" I say, "This is how our novels were meant to be—lived!" Deep POV will help the writer to draw readers into each point-of-view character's mind so thoroughly that they will feel as if they are living inside the character's skin.

Even novice writers are familiar with the concept of Point of View. Most even know the difference between first person and third person. If we're really savvy, we understand the concept of tenses—past, present, and future. However, Deep Point of View puts basic POV on steroids. The technique tightens, solidifies, and strengthens a manuscript. As a stellar side-effect, many of those pesky problems with "show/don't tell" will fade away like a bad memory.

I learned this technique from my awesome editor in the school of deadline during the substantive edit of my debut novel, *Reluctant Burglar*, and my writing has never been the same. Honestly, when she showed me the tips and tricks I wondered where I'd been all my life—or why my publisher picked up my rookie manuscript in the shape they first saw it.

My goal in the following pages is to impart that grand "light bulb" moment to other writers. Curious? Read on!

Chapter One: Point of View Basics

This chapter will establish groundwork in basic points of view, persons, and tenses, as well as definitions that will serve us throughout the book. Even if you think you know this material, I challenge you to absorb it afresh, in order to prepare yourself for the next steps.

The term *Point of View* is defined as a position from which something is considered or evaluated, a standpoint, or a place of perception. In fiction writing, the position from which anything is considered in any given scene should be the character through whose head we are viewing events. That character's psyche—his or her very soul—is the standpoint from which everything else in the scene is presented and evaluated. This particular character is the point-of-view character. For simplicity, I will refer to point of view as POV and the point-of-view character as POVC.

In order to remain firmly inside the POVC's head, nothing in a scene can be presented for reader consideration that is outside that character's awareness. When judging writing contest entries, I often see POV violations similar to:

> At a long creak from the attic above, Karen froze, heart pounding. Was that a footfall? Unaware, Karen's hold on the vase of flowers relaxed, and she dropped it.

If Karen is the POVC and isn't consciously aware that her hold on the vase slipped then it is a POV violation to mention that she dropped the vase until the very moment when she realizes her unconscious action. The segment could be rewritten like this:

Karen froze, heart pounding. Was that long creak a footfall in the attic above? She held her breath.

Crash!

Cool moisture splashed her ankles. Karen shrieked and jumped back.

That sound hadn't come from above. She gazed toward her feet at a tangle of bright blooms scattered amid shards of glass and splotches of water on the hardwood floor. Her heart sank. What a fraidy-cat she was. One little out-of-the-ordinary sound and she dropped the beautiful vase of flowers Glen had given her.

See how this sequence flows in a linear and logical fashion with only what Karen sees, knows, thinks, and experiences in the moment? We remain firmly in the *now*. We haven't run ahead of events, lagged behind, or inserted information that could only come from an invisible narrator. How much more poignant this event becomes when we stay inside the POVC's head, and how much more powerful to write it in Deep POV, as in the above segment.

Another type of POV violation I commonly see is something like this:

Bill turned away and didn't notice Chet slip out the door.

If we are in Bill's POV, and he didn't notice Chet's sneaky retreat, then the incident cannot be mentioned. So how does the writer convey to the reader that Chet has escaped? Ways exist to write this segment, maintain POV, and still make the reader aware of this vital information. Again, my "fix" will be written in Deep POV, even though it is possible to write the segment in shallow POV—telling, rather than showing—and yet avoid a POV violation. Later in the book, we'll look at before and after segments that illustrate the difference between shallow, "telling" POV and Deep POV.

Here is my rewrite:

> Fists clenching and unclenching, Bill gazed around the kitchen. Where was that louse? He had to be here somewhere.
>
> "Chet, I need to talk to you. Now!"
>
> Silence answered Bill's shout.
>
> He strode toward the living room. A gentle whoosh of air behind him stopped him in his tracks. Bill whirled. The screen door was settling back into place. The coward was on the run.

Now the reader knows that Chet slipped out the door, but we haven't left Bill's POV in order to convey that information. Plus, by refusing to take the lazy way out and "tell" the information through a POV violation, the story becomes much more immediate and exciting. Isn't the result worth the extra effort?

Other basic POV violations could include phrases like the following:

> Face flushed, eyes spitting fire . . .
>
> or
>
> Gaze crackling, a low growl rumbled from his throat.

Unfortunately for POV maintenance, the POVC cannot know that his or her eyes are "blazing" or "spitting fire". The character can't even know the color of his or her face. The character can, however, know how the flushed face *feels* or be aware of other telltale signs of anger, and that's the angle from which to approach the description.

Fixes could include something like the following:

Face hot, Heidi slammed the drawer.

or

Eyes narrowed, nostrils flared, a low growl rumbled from his throat.

Now we have remained inside the POVC's head, yet accurately portrayed the character's emotional state.

#

Next, let's take a look at the various persons in which a story can be told.

First Person

In this person, the viewpoint character is "I." A story told in first person requires that nothing can be heard, seen, or experienced except through the senses of the character relating the story.

However, a first-person narrative does allow for the viewpoint character to skip ahead in the sequence of events, and make a comment like, "If I had known . . .," because first person can have something of a diary or journal feel, but be aware that these "journaling" lines are necessarily telling rather than showing. Weigh the moment, and decide if the segue into telling is worth the loss of immediacy.

But, you protest, isn't first person automatically Deep POV? This is a common misperception, and I used to agree—until I started writing a first person manuscript. Suddenly, I discovered myself employing my entire arsenal of Deep POV techniques in order to make the story even more immediate. It is possible to write "shallow" and "telling" first person. Who knew? We will cover this issue in greater depth, complete with examples, in the final chapter.

Second Person

In this person, the viewpoint character is "you." This is a problematic and difficult POV in which to tell a

9

story. Readers want to identify with the characters in a novel; they don't necessarily want the writer's finger pointed at them as the "you" character. Lines from a book written in second person might be:

> You went to the store, but they were out of cabbage. Grumbling under your breath, you went back to your apartment and found a stranger watching television in your living room.

The above example is an intriguing situation, but an awkward presentation.

Sometimes a conversational tone in a manuscript will tempt a writer to dart into second person. For instance: Why do you never find a cab available on a Saturday night? When I find constructions like this—in my manuscripts or in manuscripts I'm judging or critiquing—I edit them out. The change in persons creates a speed-bump in readers' minds. Not a good thing! Better to say: Why were cabs so scarce on a Saturday night? This is good Deep POV and will gel fine with either first or third person.

Occasionally, second person is used in nonfiction, such as for listing step-by-step instructions or in teaching manuals like this one.

Third Person

This is the most commonly used person for storytelling. The viewpoint character is "he," "she," or occasionally "it" (if you're writing science fiction or fantasy). A third-person novel may be written in single, multiple, or omniscient points of view.

Let's look more closely at these options.

Third Person, Single POV

This choice requires the author to remain inside one character throughout the story (much like first person). Single POV creates an excellent opportunity for readers to identify with the POVC and thus be drawn into the story without switching mental gears. A drawback is the limitation in what can be shown "on stage." Events that happen outside the POVC's experience must either be told to him by another character or discovered by that character in some other way. Fortunately, there are many entertaining and engrossing approaches to deliver this "off-screen" information. We will look at some of these techniques as part of our Deep POV lessons later in the handbook.

Third Person, Multiple POV

Using this method, the writer puts the reader into the heads of more than one character during the course of the story. For instance, romances commonly employ the POVs of the male and female protagonists. In suspense, the writer might include scenes from the villain's POV, as well as the protagonist's.

A novice writer may take advantage of third person, multiple POV to hop from the head of one character to another within a single scene, intending to make sure that the reader is aware of every aspect of what is taking place and what everyone in the scene thinks about it. However, few writers are able to ping-pong around inside everyone's heads without creating confusion for the reader. Yes, I know there are best-selling writers who habitually head-hop, and a little whiny voice inside us gripes that they're getting away with things we peons can't. But then, maybe we should ask ourselves if we really want to get away with it.

When writing in third person, multiple POV powerful and effective ways exist to remain in a single POV throughout a scene and yet convey the subtleties of reaction, attitude, and emotion emanating from other characters by employing body language, voice inflection, and mannerisms. The seasoned writer can grasp this opportunity for misdirection and misunderstanding. When confined to a single character's head for at least an entire scene, it is possible for the POVC to misread the situation, and the misperception creates additional conflict valuable to the story. The POVC could perceive something about another character and have their conclusion be entirely wrong! Done right, this option provides a lot of fun for reader and writer.

Limiting yourself to a single POVC per scene or even a whole chapter is a far more effective and interesting means of weaving the story than flea-jumping from one head to another. This approach is also more respectful of your readers' intelligence and their ability to understand what is going on without the omniscient information from every character's POV. However, this technique does require that extra bit of effort, but the sweat is worth the result.

Third Person, Omniscient POV

In this POV, the viewpoint character is an omniscient narrator who tells a story about a cast of characters from an all-knowing position. The difference between this POV and head-hopping is that the narrator himself becomes an unseen character, and the story may or may not enter the heads of the other characters, leaving the god-like narrator to describe what is happening from his all-encompassing understanding. The omniscient narrator may even share with the reader details that are beyond any of the characters' knowledge.

Sweeping epics, such as J. R. R. Tolkein's *Lord of the Rings,* purposefully employ this point of view to good effect. The advantage of this POV for an epic tale is in managing the length of the story and the sheer number of characters.

#

Let's move on to the basic tenses that can be used in storytelling. There are only three: Past, Present, and Future. The following are examples of each:

Past = He went to the store.

Present = He is going to the store.

Future = He will go to the store.

Most novels are written in the past tense. The majority of readers appear most comfortable with this tense.

A few prominent writers have established a readership for their present-tense novels, but this is a harder sell to publishers. A writer attempting to break into print doesn't need any extra strikes against them. Does this mean you should change your tense if you've already written your masterpiece in present tense? Not necessarily. If you're convinced that present tense is the best choice for your novel, and you can deliver a lucid, compelling argument to support your choice, go for it! I'm merely alerting you to a practical reality of this writing journey.

I can't think of any novels written in future tense, and I'm not sure I'd care to see one. 'Nuff said.

#

To conclude this chapter, here are a few areas of common concern in regard to persons, tenses, and POV issues:

About choosing between first person and third person:

By nature, first person does create immediate intimacy with the POV character, though it is possible to enhance that immediacy with Deep POV techniques. However, take heart, you third-person scribes, Deep POV creates first-person intimacy while preserving third-person flexibility as far as the number of POV characters.

About mixing first person and third person scenes in a novel:

This is a challenging approach to storytelling and requires mature skills. I can't recommend it for a writer trying to break into print, though numerous established writers, such as Stephen King, Brandilyn Collins, and Marlo Schalesky, have used this technique effectively.

Here are a few legitimate purposes for choosing this approach:

1. To focus the story on a single major character in first person, while exploring the POVs of other characters in third person
2. To contrast the present from the past when writing lengthy flashbacks
3. To help hide the identity of the villain through brief first person scenes, while writing the rest of the story in third person

The choice to mix persons in a novel must be purposeful, rather than merely quirky.

About interspersing omniscient POV with various characters' POVs:

I've seen this done—most often in international thrillers or sprawling epics. Is the technique effective? Sometimes. If the story has "a cast of thousands" with numerous POV characters playing vital roles, omniscient is a practical tool to streamline the story. See my earlier comments in regard to omniscient POV.

If the story is smaller in scope, in my opinion the writer (and the reader) is better served by keeping the POV intimate to the main character or a select few characters. Why hold the reader at arm's length? By nature, omniscient is "telling" rather than "showing."

None of our craft should occur by happenstance. Yes, in that first draft, we may stumble upon a voice or a technique that we like, and we flow with it in creative mode. But when we arrive at editing time and have to step back—moving from right brain to left brain, if you will—we should be able to discern and verbalize, at least to ourselves, why a certain thing works or why it doesn't, and mold the story with deliberate wisdom and skill.

Here is your assignment:
The following page contains a worksheet to help you evaluate your Work in Progress (WIP) in the areas of persons, tenses, and POV options.

Basic Points of View, Persons, and Tenses Worksheet

Employing the criteria covered in Chapter One, evaluate your Work in Progress (WIP) by answering the following questions:

1. At any time, do I violate basic POV by inserting comments that the POVC cannot know?

2. What tense—past, present, or future—am I using to tell the story?

3. Why have I selected this tense? Is it best serving my story? Why or why not?

4. Do I ever slip from one tense into another, such as moving from third person into second person by use of the word "you" in my narrative?

5. What person am I using to tell the story?

6. Why did I select this person?

7. If I have chosen more than one person, does the mixture best serve my story? Why or why not?

Chapter Two: Deep POV Is/Deep POV Isn't

Deep Point of View is one of many techniques writers may deploy from their arsenal of skills in order to craft a book to their highest capabilities. In this chapter, we will examine what Deep POV is and what it isn't, in order to gain a stronger understanding of the purpose and nature of this technique.

Following is a vital term that will be used throughout the rest of the book.

Narrative Distance

Writers create narrative distance when they consciously or unconsciously insert an invisible narrator between the POVC and the reader. This issue is also known as author intrusion and is not the same as purposefully choosing omniscient POV as best suited to tell an epic tale. As this handbook progresses, I will share many examples of how we create narrative distance and how we can eliminate it in order to achieve Deep POV.

The following are some identifying characteristics of Deep POV.

1. Deep POV eliminates narrative distance.

Readers will feel like there is nothing between them and what is happening to the POVC. In Deep POV, we don't want thoughts or actions told or explained by a third party; we want to live the events inside the POVC's head. The narrative should read like the thoughts going through the character's mind but without the need to italicize as in direct thought quotations.

Following are a few examples that demonstrate what a sentence might look like with that annoying, invisible narrator buzzing in the reader's ear and then with the narrator eliminated. In future chapters, we will take a closer look at why these fixes work, as well as the techniques and principles necessary to perform these adjustments.

With the narrator: She wished she could whisk back in time and redo the last few minutes.
Without the narrator: Too bad life didn't come with an *undo* button like a computer.

With the narrator: He had to think hard about what to do next.
Without the narrator: What should he do next?

With the narrator: Jason's scowl caused Meg to sigh on the inside.
Without the narrator: If Jason's scowl turned any blacker, lightning would strike her dead. A silent sigh left Meg's lips.

2. Deep POV is always immediate.

Deep POV keeps the story anchored in the *now*. What is the POVC thinking and doing in this very moment? Deep POV is a particularly excellent choice for high action books or scenes. Or conversely, it is a wonderful way to flow in the psyche of the POV character during contemplative moments.

Here's an example of a high action segment written in Deep POV:

She darted behind the trunk of the tree, and her foot kicked something hard that skimmed into the grass. She dove after it and came up with the Beretta. Then she grabbed the rifle. Forget looking for the clip. Salvador's men were wrapping up the last of the massacre. Bodies lay everywhere. Soon the gunmen would converge on Tony if he wasn't already dead.

18

A crash came from the hut, and then a spurt of bullets and men's shouts. One of them Tony's.

Desi ran toward the hut. Her breath rasped. Blood pounded in her ears. *Please, God, let me be in time.*

(From *Reluctant Smuggler*, Book Three in my To Catch a Thief series)

Do you see how Deep POV brings the action seamlessly alive? We're inside Desi's heart and mind throughout the entire sequence.

Now here's an example of a contemplative moment written in Deep POV:

Samantha studied the profile of the man behind the wheel of the pickup. Nice strong chin, a little on the square side, but not jutting, and definitely not weak. Just right. And his hand holding hers had been just right, too, wrapping her palm and fingers in a big grip, but no squeezing.

All well and good, but why was she alone in a pickup with a guy she'd just met? She'd wanted to escape the deluge of reporters as much as Ryan, but why did she feel perfectly at home sitting here? And safe? The police maintained he wasn't a suspect in the murder case. Less than an hour ago she'd believed him capable of breaking and entering. What had changed?

The stray dog. Despite his tough exterior, the man had a core of kindness. Even her moody cat knew it and trusted him. And Sam trusted animals. They had a sense about people that human beings often didn't.

Ryan shot her a glance with his intense blue eyes, and the corners of his mouth tilted up.

What was the matter with her? She'd better quit staring or the guy would get the wrong idea.

(From *Evidence of Murder*, award-winning 2009 Steeple Hill release)

Do you see how immediate and intimate this moment feels, flowing along in the psyche of the female protagonist? And yet her thoughts are completely pertinent to her current situation, no idle woolgathering. Each sentence comes out exactly as she observes and thinks in the moment. The train of thought is linear and active, and conveys both the voice and the attitudes of the POVC. However, we need to be careful not to allow this type of contemplation to implode into dull self-absorption, which brings us to the next point.

3. Deep POV is not a long string of internal monologue.

Your narrative should not stall out with the POVC endlessly nattering to himself while nothing in particular happens around him. Action and contemplation alike should be Deep, with clear-cut comments from within the character's psyche alternating and flowing with the external activity. In Deep POV, no gulf stretches between what the character feels internally and what is going on around him. They feed off each other in smooth and dynamic rhythm.

Here's an example from *Reluctant Runaway*, Book Two in my To Catch a Thief series. The heroine, Desiree, has been abandoned in the desert, and now she's run into double trouble—a notorious motorcycle gang. Notice how her inner monologue flows naturally with the external conversation and activity—all in Deep POV.

Desi stared into the flat gray eyes of the lead motorcyclist. He wore a black denim shirt with the sleeves ripped off and the seams hanging ragged. His bronzed arms were a rolling terrain of muscle and ink. A massive pewter cross dangled from his neck on a leather cord, and a sliver of tattoo peeked from his shirt neck.

Was she face-to-face with the infamous Snake Bonney? He wasn't as big as she'd first thought, charging down on her like that. But he was no pip-squeak either. She'd be no match for him by himself, much less with the gang of hard-faced clones around him. She swallowed—or started to, but she couldn't find a drop of saliva.

A hard grin split the leader's reddish beard. "You lost?" His voice resembled his motorcycle's rumble.

"Out for a walk." Her words came out a croak. "Headed back to the road. The way you—" *cough*— "came." She coughed again and then took a quick sip from the canteen. "See?" She held up the water container. "I'm prepared."

He pointed at her headdress. "You're far out."

Desi blinked. Far out? This guy wasn't old enough to be a seventies reject. Must be some kind of Sonny Barger hero emulation. Of course, the founder of the Hell's Angels was decades older now, like the rest of the world, and probably didn't talk that way anymore either. Not a good time to point that out, but—Okay, she was thinking goofy things to keep from panicking.

"I'll be on my way now. Bye." She stepped forward.

The cycles revved . . .

Notice in the previous segment that Desiree thinks many things in an internal voice that is clearly her own,

21

but none of these thoughts require italics. This takes us to our next point.

4. Deep POV is not italicized.

Increasing the amount of italicized direct thought quotations does not transform narrative into Deep POV. The object of Deep POV is to anchor the reader inside the POVC's head without continually quoting verbatim from her mind.

Here's an example of what I mean:

> Jane looked out the window. *Wow! Look at that sunshine and the dew sparkling on the roses. What a perfect day for gardening. I'd better go get my tools.* She went to the garage and scanned her shelves. *Now, where did I put my gloves and trowel?*

In the above example, we are certainly in Jane's head—uncomfortably so—but the abundance of italics and the hip-hop between "she" and "I" will soon become tedious to the reader.

Here is an example of the same narrative written in Deep POV.

> Jane looked out the window. The dew on the roses sparkled in the morning sunlight. *Wow!* Would there ever be a better day for gardening? Humming, she hurried into the garage. Her gaze searched the wooden shelves. Where had she stored her gloves and trowel?

Deep POV does use italics for brief direct thought quotations, but no more frequently than in shallow POV. The use of italicized verbatim thoughts should be limited to exclamations or colloquialisms that require the extra emphasis of italics.

5. Deep POV will eliminate most, if not all, problems with show/don't tell.

Is anyone ready to do the happy dance? Deep POV renders "telling" nearly impossible, because that annoying, invisible narrator has been given the boot!

Following is the opening paragraph of *Calculated Revenge*, my spring 2010 release for Steeple Hill. It is written in Deep POV.

> The grimy backpack rested abandoned against the playground fence. Laney Thompson's eyes riveted on the school bag, but her feet stuck to the gravel near the swings. What was the matter with her? The students had rushed less than a minute ago into the elementary school building after noon recess. One of them must have forgotten the bag. Simple explanation. Then why did her skin pebble as if she stood on this Minnesota playground in mid-January rather than the balmy end of May?

Here's the same paragraph regressed into "telling" mode. Can you spot the flat, telling, narrator intrusion?

> Laney Thompson saw the grimy backpack resting abandoned against the playground fence. She tried to step toward it, but something kept her from moving her feet. She'd watched the students rush less than a minute ago into the elementary school building after noon recess. One of them must have forgotten the bag, she thought. She considered that a logical explanation. Yet she felt her skin pebble as if she stood on this Minnesota playground in mid-January rather than the balmy end of May.

Future chapters will examine specifics about the types of "telling" errors made in this second example and then demonstrate techniques to eliminate "tells" and stay Deep with your story.

6. Deep POV will not allow lazy characterization.

The writer must live inside the character in order to keep the reader inside the POVC's head. Maintaining that level of intimacy will require you to become saturated with every aspect of your POVC so actions and reactions become believable at a profound level.

7. Deep POV polishes the voice of the POV character.

When you write the narrative like the character would talk or think, the character's voice must shine through. Note the examples given previously in this chapter, especially the one from Desi's encounter with the motorcycle gang. Her gutsy, quirky personality glows through her inner monologue.

8. The expert user of Deep POV will know that there are times to "tell."

Even stories written primarily in Deep POV will contain times when it is a favor to the story to condense and "tell" certain types of mundane and transitional events and then "go deep" when the real action commences once more. As in all things creative, the artist must be sensitive to rhythm and balance.

The following is an example of how Deep POV can flow with the brief moments when it is time to go less deep in order to move the story along. I have italicized the key "telling" phrase in order to draw it to your attention, though the phrase would not be italicized in the manuscript.

Mom turned the vehicle into the mall parking lot. In the back seat, I sat up stiff. What? We weren't headed for the zoo? Here,

I'd been practicing that Blue Macaw whistle, so high and sweet. Today was supposed to be the day the bright bird answered my call. *A few minutes later*, I was stuck indoors, shuffling along cold tiled floors while my sister hunted for the perfect dress. Like that would ever happen.

Notice how closely we stay inside this young girl's head throughout the passage, except for that transitional phrase when I go shallow in order to move the characters from the car to the interior of the mall. By saying "a few minutes later," I eliminate paragraphs of mundane activity that could turn tedious and are unnecessary to the story. This is an example of when and how to pull back seamlessly then zoom in again.

Now, we've covered some basics of what Deep POV will do for your manuscript, as well as what it should *not* look like. Have you read books that exhibited these characteristics and that you now realize were written in Deep POV? If so, I recommend that you begin finding more such books and studying the technique. One of the best ways to learn and reinforce a new craft skill is by observing how masters do it.

If you're scratching your head about what authors this might include, I have a few recommendations. Anything by Brandilyn Collins is written in excellent Deep POV. You should also check out books by Karen Ball. She is the editor who yanked my skill level up by the bootstraps by imparting these techniques during the editorial process for my debut novel. Also, it probably goes without saying that books by me are written in Deep POV. (There, I said it!)

Here are your assignments:

1. Obtain through your library or local bookstore at least one book by an author who writes in Deep POV and read it.

2. Complete the review worksheet on the following page. All of the answers to the questions are found in these first two chapters. By completing the worksheet in your own words, you will reinforce the material in your memory.

Chapters One and Two Review Worksheet

Define Point of View:

Define First Person:

Define Second Person:

Define Third Person:

  Omniscient =

  Single =

  Multiple =

Name the Three Tenses:

Narrative Distance is:

Deep POV is:

Deep POV is not:

Is there a time to "tell"? When?

Chapter Three: Never Say He Thought/She Thought

In Deep POV, you will not need to write he thought/she thought. The same goes for he felt/she felt . . . he knew/she knew. . . wondered . . . realized . . . speculated . . . decided . . . wished . . . etc. These phrases are death to Deep POV, because they create narrative distance. Readers are now at arm's length from the character, not in the POVC's head where they belong.

A narrator is required in order to say that a character "knew" something or "felt" something or "wondered" something. Inside ourselves, we rarely preface or follow our thoughts with those kinds of words. We simply think what we think without saying to ourselves that we "thought" it or "wondered" it or "knew" it. If we are inside a certain character's psyche, why would we need to say he thought/knew/realized/felt something, etc., when we can proceed directly to whatever it was that the character thought?

Here are some examples:

Shallow POV: He thought a good bath wouldn't hurt the dog.
Deep POV: *Whew!* A good bath would do this dog a world of good.

Shallow POV: She feels a sinking sensation in her middle.
Deep POV: Her stomach drops to her toes.
(Notice this example is in present tense for the sake of variety.)

Shallow POV: He knew that if she did that, she'd fail.
Deep POV: If she did that, she'd fail.

Shallow POV: She wondered how she would get through the next day.
Deep POV: How could she possibly survive the next day?

Shallow POV: I wished I hadn't said that.
Deep POV: If only I hadn't said that.
(See how Deep POV applies to First Person too?)

In Deep POV, we get straight to the point, exactly like people would think in their heads, without the narrator commentary. As with most rules, an exception exists. It's okay to write he thought/she thought, etc., in dialogue. Example: "He thinks the dog smells," Betty said with a laugh. Or even better, "He thinks the dog smells." Betty laughed.

Here are a couple of hints for transforming those "telling" sentences into "showing" Deep POV:

1. Never underestimate the power of "if" and "if only."
2. When a statement won't do, pose a question.

How about a few more examples?

> **Shallow:** A pair of strangers approached the house, and I wondered who they could be. I felt fear grip me. It couldn't be the IRS again. I thought we'd gotten that misunderstanding straightened out.
> **Deep:** A pair of strangers in suits and ties goose-stepped up the walk toward the front door. Not the IRS again. My stomach clenched. Hadn't we gotten that little misunderstanding straightened out?

Shallow: Kendra realized she couldn't take the whole litter of puppies with her at once. She tried to think of ways she could smuggle them out one by one.

Deep: Kendra eyed the squirming, yipping mass of fur. No way could she get the whole litter of puppies out of here at once. How might she smuggle them free one by one?

Shallow: Pulling her coat tight against a frigid blast of wind, she thought she would never complain about the desert sun again.

Deep: A frigid blast of wind iced her skin, and she pulled her coat tight around her. She'd never complain about the desert sun again.

Here is your assignment:

Let's do some practice transformations. Take each "telling" sentence on the next page and move it into Deep POV by eliminating the narrator's voice. Remember the techniques we've covered so far, and don't make the changes more complicated than they need to be. I assure you, every one of these examples can be fixed with ease.

When you've finished your answers, you can check out my sample "fixes" on the pages following the worksheet. I have included these by way of example only, and do not intend to imply that they are the only ways to rephrase the sentences in Deep POV.

Chapter Three Worksheet

Shallow: He wondered whether she would show up for his birthday party.

Deep:

Shallow: I could never do that, she thought.

Deep:

Shallow: Jacob realized he was dying, and the moment made him feel strangely free.

Deep:

Shallow: Thoughts of cake and candy tormented her.

Deep:

Shallow: There was no bread or milk in the house so Mitchell decided to go to the store.

Deep:

Shallow: Mary knew he never kept his promises, so she realized she'd be an idiot to believe him now.

Deep:

Chapter Three Worksheet Sample Answers

Shallow: He wondered whether she would show up for his birthday party.

Deep: Would she even bother to show up for his birthday party?

Shallow: I could never do that, she thought.

Deep: If only she possessed the skill to pull that off.

Shallow: Jacob realized he was dying, and the moment made him feel strangely free.

Deep: So this was death. Pain vanished. All limits lifted. Why did anyone dread this moment? His spirit leaped toward his Maker.

Shallow: Thoughts of cake and candy tormented her.

Deep: No sweets. No way. No how. She wouldn't give in to temptation. *Yeah, right!* Who was she fooling?

Shallow: There was no bread or milk in the house so Mitchell decided to go to the store.

Deep: Mitchell slammed the cupboard door. No bread, and no milk either. Time to go to the store. He shrugged into his coat.

Shallow: Mary knew he never kept his promises, so she realized she'd be in idiot to believe him now.

Deep: He never kept his promises. What kind of fool would she be to believe him now?

Chapter Four: Name That Feeling—Not!

In order for our readers to live inside a character's head, they must feel what that character feels. But contrary to expectation—and the way many of us write—naming the emotion the character feels accomplishes the opposite of Deep POV. It holds the reader at arm's length and creates narrative distance by telling, rather than showing.

Study the Shallow (telling) and Deep samples below. The first one is from my debut novel, *Reluctant Burglar*. Notice the dramatic difference between my original manuscript and the published version.

> **Shallow** (from my raw manuscript): Tony closed his phone, frustration and fury surging through him.

What's wrong with this? Surging is a strong verb, isn't it? Yes and no. An "ing" version of a verb waters down its power, but I've compounded the issue by "telling" the reader how Tony feels, rather than creating a word picture that "shows" the emotion in power-house Deep POV.

> **Deep** (from the published version): Tony slapped the phone shut. If steam could escape out his pores, he'd be a toxic cloud.

Whoo-hoo! Now we're right there inside Tony. No need to name the emotion. We feel that frustration and fury in our pores too.

In the examples below, note how the statement of emotion in the Shallow version is supported by a stout verb, and yet the Deep example emerges more powerful and emotionally evocative.

> **Shallow:** Joy rocketed through Adrienne.
> **Deep:** A grin the size of the big, blue sky stretched Adrienne's lips. If her feet met the sidewalk, they sure didn't know it.

> **Shallow:** Despair tugged at Jenny's heart. No one ever believed her.
> **Deep:** Jenny wilted into her chair. What was the point of trying to defend herself?

> **Shallow:** Hot jealousy flashed through me.
> **Deep:** Heat boiled my insides. If that wimp could win a trophy, where was mine?

Do you see how the prose is enriched by refusing to dictate to the reader what the POV character feels? How often do we think in our heads, "I feel angry right now"? Or, "I'm full of joy"? No, we generally don't name the emotion; we simply feel it and behave accordingly. Emotions have several effects that the Deep POV writer can capitalize on in order to convey the feeling without naming it.

1. **Physical effects on the body that can be described**. If a character is angry, his hands might form fists. Or if a character is overjoyed she might sweep her arms high and shout or laugh. If nervous, his palms might sweat, or if truly afraid, his throat might close. Any natural physical reaction that might occur in response to a certain emotion is fair game for your Deep POV narrative.

2. **Thoughts in keeping with that particular emotion**. For instance, if a character is bitter and angry, a line of narrative could be something like: Why did he always end up on the trash heap? Or if a character is

anticipating something, a line might read: I'd give my last nickel for the clock to move faster. These are the character's actual thoughts expressed in narrative without the need to italicize, and the words accurately and powerfully reflect what the character feels without the need to bop the reader over the head by naming the emotion. By its very nature, Deep POV respects your reader's intelligence, and they will thank you for the courtesy.

3. **Actions and behaviors.** For instance, an angry character might throw something across the room or slam a drawer. A stressed-out character may exhibit a mannerism that you've built into your character, such as the need to go bake something, or even biting her nails or twisting her hair around her finger, though these last two suggestions are fairly humdrum. Strive to avoid cliché mannerisms while taking advantage of these opportunities to employ something unique to your character's personality.

Here is your assignment:

The next two pages contain "telling" sentences for you to transform into dazzling Deep POV. As you rewrite the sentences, *be watchful to remain in the same person as the sample sentence.* If the "shallow" sentence is in First Person, your Deep POV sentence should be also. If the "shallow" sentence is Third Person, remain in Third Person in your Deep POV version. Remember, simply changing narrative into First Person from Third is not what creates Deep POV! Also, for this exercise, *do not insert dialogue.* We want to learn how to transform our narrative from tell to dramatic show.

After you've done the exercise, you can check out my sample answers on the page following your worksheet.

Chapter Four Worksheet

Remember that you're writing the narrative as if you're inside the character's head. The particular point of this exercise is to avoid naming the emotion, but convey it through:

1. physical effects on the body that can be described
2. thoughts in keeping with that particular emotion
3. actions and behaviors

BONUS TIP: Rewording the sentence but continuing to name the emotion or one of its synonyms or derivatives does not add up to Deep POV!

Shallow: Annoyed, Heidi slammed the drawer.

Deep:

Shallow: Disappointment at Allan's absence dulled my enthusiasm for the outing.

Deep:

Shallow: Fear caused my palms to sweat and my heart rate to soar.

Deep:

Shallow: He took the turn faster than good sense allowed, fury lashing him onward.

Deep:

Shallow: The more Collin thought about the snub, the more aggravated he became.

Deep:

Shallow: Joy turned her insides into a song.

Deep:

Chapter Four Worksheet Sample Answers

Shallow: Annoyed, Heidi slammed the drawer.

Deep: Grumbling under her breath, Heidi slammed the drawer. Who took the keys?

Shallow: Disappointment at Allan's absence dulled my enthusiasm for the outing.

Deep: Why bother going if Allan wasn't coming along?

Shallow: Fear caused my palms to sweat and my heart rate to soar.

Deep: I wiped sweaty palms on my jeans and swallowed my fluttering heart into place.

Shallow: He took the turn faster than good sense allowed, fury lashing him onward.

Deep: He whipped the wheel of the car to the left and skidded into the turn. Sure, he was nuts to speed on these roads, but that woman drove him insane. Certifiable!

Shallow: The more Collin thought about the snub, the more aggravated he became.

Deep: Collin scowled. What right did she have to ignore him?

Shallow: Joy turned her insides into a song.

Deep: The *Hallelujah Chorus* swept through her heart.

Chapter Five: Ditch Prepositional Tells

What is a "prepositional tell"? I coined this phrase to describe how Deep POV is often destroyed when we attach little phrases to our narrative that begin with a preposition (of, with, in, etc.) and then go on to name an emotion, an attitude, or a thought. This habit that we so easily fall into turns the narrative into "telling" rather than "showing."

Below are a couple of examples from my raw manuscript for *Reluctant Burglar,* followed by the published version. For emphasis, I italicized the telling prepositional phrases. The phrases were not italicized in the manuscript.

> **Shallow**: Desiree's skin prickled *with pleasant excitement.*
> **Deep**: Shadows loomed. The place reeked of ancient secrets. Desi's skin prickled.

See how the Deep version is more alive and intriguing? We don't have to tell the reader that Desi is energized by this atmosphere. The reader can see that for themselves and actively enter into what she feels.

> **Shallow:** "I agreed to your examination of the piece to silence any doubts. I am confident your suspicion will prove unfounded." He lifted his chin *with a hint of stubborn defiance.*
> **Deep:** "I agreed to your examination of the piece to silence any doubts. I am confident your suspicion will prove unfounded." He lifted his chin.

The prepositional phrase in the Shallow sentence was unnecessary. The reader understands the attitude by the context without being hit with the information like a pie in the face. Don't be afraid of this sort of subtlety in your storytelling. Your readers will appreciate your respect for their intelligence.

NOTE: I'm not saying that prepositions should be eliminated from our Deep POV manuscripts. That would be impossible and extremely awkward. Prepositions are necessary in narrative, but not to convey the character's thoughts, emotions, or attitudes. Those should be shown in Deep POV. (See? I used several prepositions in this explanation.)

So how do we go about eliminating prepositional tells? Here are a few hints to help you along.

Rely on context.

Oh, and be sure to rely on context.

Employ the writer's "showing" arsenal: physical effects that can be described, thoughts, actions, behavior, and dialogue.

Did I mention that it's vital to rely on context? ;-)

Here are a few more examples:

Shallow: Desiree eyed the paper *with satisifaction.*

Deep: Plate shoved the form across the desk toward her. Desiree grinned on the inside. *Gotcha!*

Which one is a blah tell, and which one showcases Desi's sassy, smart, and savvy personality?

Shallow: She narrowed her eyes in comprehension.

Deep (in the context of the conversation): "What gives, girl? You don't often get that look on your face. Like a cross between a mule and bronco. Last time was when that hot Italian agent came around and . . . ohhhhh . . ." She narrowed cat-green eyes then laughed. "Tall, dark, and intense musta been

41

hangin' around again. And he missed you? What a hoot!"

Can you see how the context makes the explanation of "comprehension" redundant and unnecessary?

Here is your assignment:
For the Shallow and Deep exercises on the next page, you are permitted and even encouraged to employ dialogue or extremely brief snippets of direct thought (like my *Gotcha!* example above) in order to transform each prepositional tell into a Deep POV show. Remember all the tools and techniques we've used in prior lessons!

As usual, my sample answers will be found on the page following your worksheet.

Chapter Five Worksheet

Shallow: He writhed in agony.

Deep:

Shallow: With smug satisfaction, he turned in the perfect paper.

Deep:

Shallow: She knew the past had caught up with her and let out a sigh of regret.

Deep:

Shallow: A growl of anger burst from my throat. "Megan, get back here!" A wave of indignation washed over me. I wasn't about to let her walk away without giving me an explanation.

Deep:

Shallow: She sang in glorious exultation.

Deep:

Chapter Five Worksheet Sample Answers

Shallow: He writhed in agony.

Deep: Crying out, he doubled over and crumpled to the ground. Fangs of fire gnawed on his insides.

Shallow: With smug satisfaction, he turned in the perfect paper.

Deep: He smirked and dropped the paper onto the teacher's desk. *Shazam!* Let's see Mr. Perfectionist give him anything less than an "A" on this one.

Shallow: She knew the past had caught up with her and let out a sigh of regret.

Deep: "I'm so sorry." She'd give anything to alter the past. A sigh crept past her lips.

Shallow: A growl of anger burst from my throat. "Megan, get back here!" A wave of indignation washed over me. I wasn't about to let her walk away without giving me an explanation.

Deep: A growl burst from my throat. "Meghan, get back here!" How dare she walk away without a word of explanation?

Shallow: She sang in glorious exultation.

Deep: Buoyant notes bubbled from her throat.

44

Chapter Six: He Saw/She Saw—Let's Get Off the See-Saw

In this chapter, I will show you how to root out and transform sensory tells into Deep POV. Saying he saw/he smelled-heard-tasted, etc. is almost never necessary in Deep POV. Instead of saying "he saw" something, simply say what he saw!

Here's an example of a sensory tell:

> He could see the tip of the dog's nose peeking out of the closet.

That sentence sounds okay, right? Why is it shallow POV? "He could see . . ." Congratulations, your character has a healthy pair of eyes. This phrase communicates mundane and obvious information, while neatly inserting the dreaded narrative distance. The fact that the POV character saw whatever he's describing is understood by the reader without being told—unless, of course, your character is blind, and then we're writing about a miracle!

Here's a Deep POV variation on the example sentence:

> Barry stepped through the door and scanned the room. The tip of the dog's nose peeked out of the closet. *Ahah!* He'd found the little critter.

Boom! Straight to the point. The verb is active, not watered down with "ing" or an "ly" adverb. And we've eliminated "could" and "saw", which are wasted words. If your reader already knows in whose POV the scene is written, why would you need to explain who is seeing what?

Here are a few more examples:

Shallow: He heard a door creak down the hall and froze in his tracks.
Deep: A door creaked down the hall, and he froze in his tracks.

Shallow: She smelled the burning bacon.
Deep: An acrid odor tainted the air. *Oh, no!* She'd left the bacon on the stove.

Shallow: The cat's fur felt silky beneath her fingertips.
Deep: The cat's silken fur slid beneath her fingertips.

Shallow: He tasted bile.
Deep: Sour bile seared his tongue.

Here is your assignment:

Let's do a few exercises where you remove the sensory "tell" and simply say whatever was seen/felt/tasted/heard/smelled. I've offered one practice exercise for each of the five senses. Look for the simplest solution to remove the sensory tell and replace it with Deep POV. None of these should require more than a sentence or two to fix. As usual, my sample answers can be found following the worksheet.

Chapter Six Worksheet

Shallow: He heard the bat connect with the ball.

Deep:

Shallow: Abigail fell forward and felt the cement of the sidewalk smack her palm.

Deep:

Shallow: She smelled the cake baking in the oven.

Deep:

Shallow: Bill saw them get out of the car and head straight for him. His stomach clenched.

Deep:

Shallow: She tasted dirt in her mouth.

Deep:

Chapter Six Worksheet Sample Answers

Shallow: He heard the bat connect with the ball.

Deep: *Crack!* Bat met ball.

Shallow: Abigail fell forward and felt the cement of the sidewalk smack her palm.

Deep: Abigail tumbled forward, and her palms smacked cement. Raw burn drew a hiss from her throat.

Shallow: She smelled the cake baking in the oven.

Deep: *Mmmm!* Cake in the oven, such a sweet birthday aroma.

Shallow: Bill saw them get out of the car and head straight for him. He felt his stomach clench.

Deep: Two burly men exited the car and headed straight for him. Bill's gut twisted.

Shallow: She tasted dirt in her mouth.

Deep: Pungent earth coated her tongue, and she spat then spat again. *Yuck!* There'd better not be any worms in this dirt.

Chapter Seven: Write Lively, Linear Prose

Several times I have mentioned the importance of writing linear narrative. Effective Deep POV demands that you take your readers through the experiences of your POVC, step-by-step, as if they reside within the character. Don't run ahead. Don't lag behind. Remain ever in the *now*!

Tying the Past and the Future to the Present

Does linear writing and remaining in the *now* mean your character can never think about or discuss the past or anticipated future events? Not at all. In our everyday lives don't we think about the past or discuss the future? Yes, but we do that thinking and discussing in the context of the present . . . the *now*.

Again, let's resort to example in order to illustrate what I mean. Here's a snippet from my fall 2010 release, *Legacy of Lies*. Rich Hendricks is thinking about his own past, as well as a past trauma in the community where he serves as police chief, but the issues arise only because they are pertinent to his present situation, and he evaluates the bygone events from the perspective of the present.

> Police Chief Rich Hendricks caught the coded call-out from the dispatcher on his police scanner at home. He immediately phoned the station for details not given over the radio, and then abandoned his half-eaten, fast-food cheeseburger. Small loss. No fun scarfing down meals alone all the time anyway. With his wife, Karen, having passed away three years ago, and his daughter, Katrina,

newly graduated and off to summer Bible camp as a counselor, life had turned pretty blah. A case like this broke up the routine big-time, but it wasn't the kind of excitement he welcomed.

A baby's bones found in a trench? When he took the chief job here in Ellington, he researched the town, particularly the criminal history. This little burg hadn't had a mystery this big since Simon Elling's son was kidnapped in 1957 and never recovered. Had the child just been found? And in the Kellers' backyard, no less!

Next here's a situation where a character is thinking about a future event, and waffling between anticipation and dread—all in Deep POV.

Ryan's chuckle warmed her ear. "See you on Saturday then."

"I'm salivating for that steak. Medium rare."

"Yes, ma'am. You just made my job easy. That's the way I like mine too."

They hung up, laughing. Samantha sobered, staring at the phone. Had Davidson meant the remark as a sign of compatibility? *Uh-oh!* He might claim he wanted to keep things casual, but did he mean it? And what about Larry and his family? Ryan said he was inviting them. Were they still coming, or was the evening going to be just the two of them?

She should call back and make some excuse. Her hand closed around the receiver then she released it as if scalded.

(from *Evidence of Murder*)

50

In both of these examples, the character is thinking about or discussing either a past event or a future plan in such a way that it is pertinent to the *now* and moves the story forward.

Fire That Lazy Sentence Construction!

Another common issue is the tendency to try to compress current events through lazy sentence constructions like such and such "made" or "caused" the character to react in such and such a way. If you hold yourself to the standard of active prose in the *now* provided by Deep POV, you will avoid slipping into this kind of limp "telling" mode.

Here are a few Shallow and Deep examples to help clarify this point.

> **Shallow:** Seth let out a sneeze, and the loud noise in my ear made me jump.
> **Deep:** *Kerchew!* I jumped like Seth had jabbed me with a stick rather than just about sneezed my ear off.

> **Shallow:** The unwashed carrot gave her mouth a tang of dirt.
> **Deep:** She chomped a bite from the carrot. Bitter grit ground between her teeth. *Ewww!* She glared at the yellow spear in her hand. Who forgot to wash the vegetables?

> **Shallow:** The hot, stuffy air caused my head to spin.
> **Deep:** The heavy air wrapped me in cellophane. A sauna would be less stifling. Every thought wilted in my brain—shriveled like my last hope of a breeze.

See how much more interesting and active are the Deep examples? The event—the sneeze, the bite, the stifling heat—occurs, and then we hear exactly how the

POVC reacts and thinks about the event, all in proper order and with a lovely savor of voice. That's Deep POV as opposed to dull "telling" mode.

Halt MRU Violations!

Did you know that MRU violations are mortal enemies of linear prose? You may never have heard of an MRU, but I guarantee that you write with them all the time.

Motivation/Reaction Units are the basic building blocks of our sentences. Placing your MRUs in proper order is critical for writing smooth and comprehensible prose for your readers—in other words, remaining linear by stating cause first and then the effect.

An MRU violation is something like putting the cart before the horse. In our sentences, we must give the motivation for a response before we state the response, and yet I see that poor old horse trotting behind the cart time and time again in contest and critique manuscripts.

> **Violation:** Nathan's hip stung after he slid into base.
> **Proper MRU:** Nathan skidded on his side toward the base. His hip stung like fire ants had crawled up his jeans. Then the umpire yelled *Safe!*, and the pain melted into oblivion.

> **Violation:** She turned on the lights when she went inside.
> **Proper MRU:** She went inside and turned on the lights.
> (Unless she is performing some unusual physical contortion, she must go inside before she turns on the lights. In the violation sentence, "when" indicates that the actions were simultaneous.)

> **Violation:** Before giving Jim the award, the principal shook his hand.

52

Proper MRU: Jim's hand was enveloped in a firm grip, and then the principal smiled and presented him the award.

Why not write that last sentence in the following way?

The principal shook Jim's hand before giving him the award.

Yes, the motivation and reaction are in the correct order in the above sentence, but now we've darted from Deep POV into omniscient POV, and that annoying, external narrator has started dictating the order of events. This is another type of "prepositional tell," when a prepositional phrase is used to yank us out of the *now*. If we are flowing along in Jim's psyche, he's not going to think "so and so did such and such *before* doing this other thing." Jim's thoughts will remain in the moment, moving smoothly from event to event, not predicting before and after moments.

An exception to this rule is "as" or "when," but only if referring to events that are truly simultaneous and perceived or experienced by the POVC at the exact same time.

For instance:

As the ball soared toward me, I lifted my bat.

or

When the receding vehicle had dimmed to a speck on the horizon, I turned away, shoulders slumped.

Here is your assignment:

Try your hand at fixing a few linear and MRU issues on the following worksheet. My sample fixes can be found after the worksheet.

53

Chapter Seven Worksheet

Shallow: I realized my cell phone was missing after I took out the trash.

Deep:

Shallow: Jenny answered the doorbell when it rang.

Deep:

Shallow: She laughed at the scowl on her friend's face.

Deep:

Shallow: The nurse's sharp look caused me to squirm in my chair.

Deep:

Shallow: He squealed and grabbed his foot in both hands as the bowling ball fell on it.

Deep:

Chapter Seven Worksheet Sample Answers

Shallow: I realized my cell phone was missing after I took out the trash.

Deep: I patted my pockets, but they were empty. No cell phone. My stomach lurched. I just took out the trash. Was my lifeline to the world wallowing in the goop of last night's discarded casserole?

Shallow: Jenny answered the doorbell when it rang.

Deep: The doorbell rang, and Jenny jerked. Inhaling a long breath, she hustled toward the foyer.

Shallow: She laughed at the scowl on her friend's face.

Deep: Her friend's simian scowl dragged a reluctant chuckle from her lips.

Shallow: The nurse's sharp look caused me to squirm in my   chair.

Deep: The nurse glared at me over the top of the counter, and I squirmed in my chair.

Shallow: He squealed and grabbed his foot in both hands as the bowling ball fell on it.

Deep: The bowling ball slipped from his grasp and landed on his toes. Hopping on one leg, he squealed and grabbed his throbbing foot in both hands.

Chapter Eight: First Person Deep Point of View

In Chapter One, I mentioned applying Deep POV techniques to first person manuscripts and promised further discussion on the subject. In this chapter I will keep my promise and simultaneously provide a review of all the principles we have covered in this handbook.

Since example is one of the most effective teaching tools, we'll move straight into the opening paragraph of *Sweet Bye-Bye,* an unpublished manuscript written in first person Deep POV.

> I found the first body a stone's throw from the colony. More littered the sun-dried grass. Pestilence or war? My heart fisted as I cradled the remains in my gloved hand and studied the brown-striped body. A sigh heaved between my lips and fluttered the veil of my bee hood. Not disease, thankfully, but someone had scampered away from the colony with a piece of this brave soldier, and a swarm of others, embedded in his flesh.

Here's what the paragraph might look like in first person Shallow POV:

> With a sense of growing dread, I spotted the first body a stone's throw from the colony. Looking around, I could see more littering the sun-dried grass. Did they die from pestilence or war? I wondered. I felt my heart fist as I cradled the remains in my gloved hand and studied the brown-

striped body. The veil of my bee hood fluttered when I heaved a sigh of relief. I was glad that the cause of death wasn't disease, but I knew someone had scampered away from the colony with a piece of this brave soldier, and a swarm of others, embedded in his flesh.

The shallow, "telling" paragraph commits every Deep POV violation that has been discussed in this handbook, proving that first person does not in and of itself eliminate that pesky narrator and guarantee Deep POV. Let's dissect the paragraph and identify each violation contrasted with the Deep version. Some of the "telling" sentences contain multiple problems.

Deep POV: I found the first body a stone's throw from the colony.
Shallow POV: *With a sense of growing dread*, I found the first body a stone's throw from the colony.

The italicized phrase illustrates a prepositional tell. The state of mind or emotion of the POVC is "told" through one of the handy, dandy prepositional phrases we like to tack onto our sentences to make sure the reader "gets" what the POV character is feeling or thinking. In this case, the prepositional phrase also waters down what would otherwise be a stark and powerful first sentence that sets the tone for the entire book. As if that were not sufficient insult to the opening line, the placement of the phrase violates the principle of linear prose. We should not indicate to our reader what the POVC is feeling or thinking or doing before we have delivered the cause for that thought, feeling, or action. Think cause and effect always!

Deep: More littered the sun-dried grass.

Shallow: Looking around, I could see more littering the sun-dried grass.

Congratulations! My POVC has an operative sense of sight. No miracle here, though, just a clumsy and unnecessary bit of telling. By cluttering up the sentence with unnecessary words, we steal punch from the stark statement in the Deep POV version.

Deep: Pestilence or war?
Shallow: Did they die from pestilence or war? I wondered.

Redundant. Redundant. Redundant. Er, did I say redundant? Doesn't the question mark at the end of the Deep POV sentence automatically indicate that the POVC is wondering something? Why tack on the telling phrase, *I wondered*, courtesy of that sneaky narrator?

Deep: My heart fisted as I cradled the remains in my gloved hand and studied the brown-striped body.
Shallow: *I felt* my heart fist as I cradled the remains in my gloved hand and studied the brown-striped body.

If a person's heart fists, don't we realize that the person feels it? This is understood information. Why do we need to tell the reader that the character felt this physical manifestation of emotion? In a very real sense, we insult our reader's intelligence by insisting on pointing out the obvious.

Deep: A sigh heaved between my lips and fluttered the veil of my bee hood.
Shallow: The veil of my bee hood fluttered when I heaved a sigh of gratitude.

Here is a classic example of an MRU violation. The sigh must be heaved before the bee hood can flutter. And again we see a prepositional tell bopping the reader over the head with the POVC's emotional response.

> **Deep:** Not disease, thankfully, but someone had scampered away from the colony with a piece of this brave soldier, and a swarm of others, embedded in his flesh.
>
> **Shallow:** I was *glad* that the cause of death wasn't disease, but *I knew* someone had scampered away from the colony with a piece of this brave soldier, and a swarm of others, embedded in his flesh.

Again, we are "telling" the emotion (gladness) instead of showing it. In contrast, the Deep POV example uses the phrase: *Not disease, thankfully* . . . This way, the reader not only understands the sense of gratitude but the character's conversational voice shines through. This type of phraseology helps the reader settle in comfortably with a character they are only beginning to know. Then lastly, the unnecessary phrase, *I knew,* continues the unfortunate trend of smacking the reader over the head with the obvious.

This examination of a single paragraph from a first person manuscript proves that first person is no more immune to shallow and telling POV than any other person in novel-writing. I have also used this exercise in comparing and contrasting Deep and Shallow versions of the same paragraph in order to review and reinforce every lesson delivered throughout this handbook.

Please see the next page for a means to contact me with any questions or comments.

Contact the Author

I've thrown a lot of information at you in this brief handbook on writing in Deep Point of View. I trust the exercises and examples have helped you grasp the principles.

If you have questions or comments, feel free to shoot me an email through my website contact page: http://www.jillelizabethnelson.com/contact.html.

I look forward to hearing from you.

Novels by Jill Elizabeth Nelson

Reluctant Burglar
(Book 1 in the To Catch a Thief series)

Reluctant Runaway
(Book 2 in the To Catch a Thief series)

Reluctant Smuggler
(Book 3 in the To Catch a Thief series)

Evidence of Murder

Witness to Murder

Calculated Revenge

Legacy of Lies

Mistletoe Mayhem
(novella in collection entitled *Season of Danger*)

For more information about Jill, her books, and her availability to speak to writers and readers groups, as well as church and civic organizations, go to www.jillelizabethnelson.com.

38523088R00037

Made in the USA
Lexington, KY
13 January 2015